Contents

Introduction

Characters are one of the most fascinating and fun parts of learning Chinese, and people are often surprised by how much they enjoy being able to write them. Added to that, *writing* the characters is also an excellent way of *learning* them. This book shows you how to write 100 of the most common characters and gives you plenty of space to practice writing them. You'll be learning a writing system which is one of the oldest in the world and which is now used by more than a billion people around the globe every day.

In this introduction we'll talk about:
- how the characters developed;
- the difference between traditional and simplified characters;
- what "radicals" are and why they're useful;
- how to count the writing strokes that are used to form each character;
- how to look up characters in a dictionary;
- how words are created by joining two characters together; and, most importantly;
- how to write the characters!

Also, in case you're using this book on your own without a teacher, we'll tell you how to get the most out of using it.

Chinese characters are not nearly as strange and complicated as people seem to think. They're actually no more mysterious than musical notation, which most people can master in only a few months. So there's really nothing to be scared of or worried about: everyone can learn them—it just requires a bit of patience and perseverance. There are also some things which you may have heard about writing Chinese characters that aren't true. In particular, you don't need to use a special brush to write them (a ball-point pen is fine), and you don't need to be good at drawing (in fact you don't even need to have neat handwriting, although it helps!)

How many characters are there?
Thousands! You would probably need to know something like two thousand to be able to read Chinese newspapers and books, but you don't need anything like that number to read a menu, go shopping or read simple street signs and instructions. Just as you can get by in most countries knowing about a hundred words of the local language, so too you can get by in China quite well knowing a hundred common Chinese characters. And this would

also be an excellent basis for learning to read and write Chinese.

How did the characters originally develop?
Chinese characters started out as pictures representing simple objects, and the first characters originally resembled the things they represented. For example:

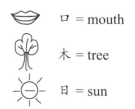

口 = mouth

木 = tree

日 = sun

Some other simple characters were pictures of "ideas":

一 one   二 two   三 three

Some of these characters kept this "pictographic" or "ideographic" quality about them, but others were gradually modified or abbreviated until many of them now look nothing like the original objects or ideas.

Then, as words were needed for things which weren't easy to draw, existing characters were "combined" to create new characters. For example, 女 (meaning "woman") combined with 子 (meaning "child") gives a new character 好 (which means "good" or "to be fond of").

Notice that when two characters are joined together like this to form a new character, they get squashed together and deformed slightly. This is so that the new, combined character will fit into the same size square or "box" as each of the original two characters. For example the character 日 "sun" becomes thinner when it is the left-hand part of the character 時 "time"; and it becomes shorter when it is the upper part of the character 星 "star". Some components got distorted and deformed even more than this in the combining process: for example when the character 人 "man" appears on the left-hand side of a complex character it gets compressed into 亻, like in the character 他 "he".

So you can see that some of the simpler characters often act as basic "building blocks" from which more complex characters are formed. This means that if you learn how to write these simple characters you'll also be learning how to write some complex ones too.

THE FIRST 100 CHINESE CHARACTERS

TRADITIONAL CHARACTER EDITION

The Quick and Easy Method to Learn the
100 Most Basic Chinese Characters

Introduction by
Alison & Lawrence Matthews

TUTTLE PUBLISHING
Tokyo • Rutland, Vermont • Singapore

Published by Tuttle Publishing, an imprint of Periplus Editions (HK) Ltd, with editorial offices at 364 Innovation Drive, North Clarendon, Vermont 05759 and 130 Joo Seng Road, #06-01, Singapore 368357.

ISBN-10: 0-8048-3832-1
ISBN-13: 978-0-8048-3832-0

Distributed by:

Japan
Tuttle Publishing
Yaekari Building 3F
5-4-12 Osaki, Shinagawa-ku
Tokyo 141-0032, Japan
Tel: (03) 5437 0171
Fax: (03) 5437 0755
Email: tuttle-sales@gol.com

North America, Latin America & Europe
Tuttle Publishing
364 Innovation Drive
North Clarendon, VT 05759-9436
Tel: (802) 773 8930
Fax: (802) 773 6993
Email: info@tuttlepublishing.com
www.tuttlepublishing.com

Asia-Pacific
Berkeley Books Pte Ltd
130 Joo Seng Road, 06-01/03
Singapore 368357
Tel: (65) 6280 1330
Fax: (65) 6280 6290
Email: inquiries@periplus.com.sg
www.periplus.com

Indonesia
PT Java Books Indonesia
Kawasan Industri Pulogadung
Jl. Rawa Gelam IV No. 9
Jakarta 13930, Indonesia
Telp. (021) 4682 1088
Fax. (021) 461 0207
Email: cs@javabooks.co.id

09 08 07 06
8 7 6 5 4 3 2 1

Printed in Singapore

How are characters read and pronounced?

The pronunciations in this workbook refer to modern standard Chinese. This is the official language of China and is also known as "Mandarin" or "putonghua".

The pronunciation of Chinese characters is written out with letters of the alphabet using a system called "Hanyu Pinyin"—or "pinyin" for short. This is the modern system used in China. In pinyin some of the letters have a different sound than in English—but if you are learning Chinese you'll already know this. We could give a description here of how to pronounce each sound, but it would take up a lot of space—and this workbook is about writing the characters, not pronouncing them! In any case, you really need to hear a teacher (or tapes) say the sounds out loud to get an accurate idea of what they sound like.

Each Chinese character is pronounced using only one syllable. However, in addition to the syllable, each character also has a particular *tone*, which refers to how the pitch of the voice is used. In standard Chinese there are four different tones, and in pinyin the tone is marked by placing an accent mark over the vowel as follows:

> 1st tone (high, flat) **mā**
> 2nd tone (rising) **má**
> 3rd tone (down-up) **mǎ**
> 4th tone (falling) **mà**

The pronunciation of each character is therefore a combination of a syllable and a tone. There are only a small number of available syllables in Chinese, and so many characters share the same syllable—in fact many characters share the same sound plus tone combination. They are like the English words "here" and "hear"—when they are spoken, you can only tell which is which from the context.

Apart from putonghua (modern standard Chinese), another well-known type of Chinese is Cantonese, which is spoken in southern China and in many Chinese communities around the world. In fact there are several dozen different Chinese languages, and the pronunciations of Chinese characters in these languages are all very different from each other. But the important thing to realize is that the characters themselves do *not* change. So two Chinese people who can't understand one other when they're talking together, can write to one another without any problem at all!

Simplified and traditional characters

As more and more characters were introduced over the years by combining existing characters, some of them became quite complicated. Writing them required many strokes which was time-consuming, and it became difficult to distinguish some of them, especially when the writing was small. So when writing the characters quickly in hand-written form, many people developed short-cuts and wrote them in a more simplified form. In the middle of the 20th century, the Chinese decided to create a standardised set of simplified characters to be used by everyone in China. This resulted in many of the more complicated characters being given simplified forms, making them much easier to learn and to write. Today in China, and also in Singapore, these simplified characters are used almost exclusively, and many Chinese no longer learn the old traditional forms. However the full traditional forms continue to be used in Taiwan and in overseas Chinese communities around the world.

Here are some examples of how some characters were simplified:

Traditional		Simplified
見	→	见
飯	→	饭
號	→	号
幾	→	几

Modern standard Chinese uses only simplified characters. But it is useful to be able to recognize the traditional forms as they are still used in many places outside China, and of course older books and inscriptions were also written using the traditional forms. In this workbook, if a character has been simplified, then its traditional form is shown in a separate box on the right-hand side of the page so that you can see what it looks like. Where no traditional form is given the character was considered simple enough already and was left unchanged.

How is Chinese written?

Chinese was traditionally written from top to bottom in columns beginning on the right-hand side of the page and working towards the left, like this:

幸福一點兒也不
難擁有。祇要妳
常為人着想，帶
來歡樂，妳會發
覺到那也是一種
幸福呀
！

This means that for a book printed in this way, you start by opening it at (what Westerners would think of as) the back cover. While writing in columns is sometimes considered archaic, you will still find many books, especially novels and more serious works of history, printed in this way.

Nowadays, though, most Chinese people write from left to right in horizontal lines working from the top of a page to the bottom, just as we do in English.

Are Chinese characters the same as English words?
Although each character has a meaning, it's not really true that an individual character is equivalent to an English "word". Each character is actually only a single *syllable*. In Chinese (like in English) some words are just one syllable, but most words are made up of two or more syllables joined together. The vast majority of words in Chinese actually consist of two separate characters placed together in a pair. These multi-syllable words are often referred to as "compounds", and this workbook provides a list of common compounds for each character.

Some Chinese characters are one-syllable words on their own (like the English words "if" and "you"), while other characters are only ever used as one half of a word (like the English syllables "sen" and "tence"). Some characters do both: they're like the English "light" which is happy as a word on its own, but which also links up to form words like "headlight" or "lighthouse".

The Chinese write sentences by stringing characters together in a long line from left to right (or in a column from top to bottom), with equal-sized spaces between each character. If English were written this way—as individual syllables rather than as words that are joined together—it would mean all the syllables would be written separately with spaces in between them, something like this:

If you can un der stand this sen tence you can read Chi nese too.

So in theory, you can't see which characters are paired together to form words, but in practice, once you know a bit of Chinese, you can!

Punctuation was not traditionally used when writing Chinese, but today commas, periods (full stops), quotation marks, and exclamation points are all used along with other types of punctuation which have been borrowed from English.

Two ways of putting characters together
We have looked at *combining characters* together to make new *characters*, and *pairing characters* together to make *words*. So what's the difference?

Well, when two simple characters are combined to form a new complex *character*, they are squashed or distorted so that the new character fits into the same size square as the original characters. The meaning of the new character *may* be related to the meaning of its components, but it frequently appears to have no connection with them at all! The new complex character also has a single-syllable pronunciation, which may or may not come from one of its parts. For example:

女	也	她
nǚ	**yě**	**tā**
woman	also	she

日	月	明
rì	**yuè**	**míng**
sun	moon/month	bright

On the other hand, when characters are *paired together* to create *words*, the characters are simply written one after the other, full sized, with a normal space in between (and there are no hyphens or anything to show that these characters are working together as a pair). The resulting word has a pronunciation which is *two* syllables—in fact it is simply the pronunciations of the individual characters one after the other. Also, you're much more likely to be able to guess the meaning of the word from the meanings of the individual characters that make it up. For example:

大	人	大人
dà	**rén**	**dàrén**
big	person	adult

姐	妹	姐妹
jiě	**mèi**	**jiěmèi**
older sister	younger sister	sisters

四	月	四月
sì	**yuè**	**sìyuè**
four	moon/month	April

Is it necessary to learn words as well as characters?
As we've said, the meaning of a compound word is often related to the meanings of the individual characters. But this is not always the case, and sometimes the word takes on a new and very specific meaning. So to be able to read a sentence and understand what it means, it isn't enough just to learn individual character—you'll also need to learn words. (In fact, a few individual characters have very little meaning at all by themselves, and only contribute to the meanings of words).

Here are some examples of common Chinese words where the meaning of the overall word is not what you might expect from the meanings of the individual characters:

明	天	明天
míng	**tiān**	**míngtiān**
bright	day/sky	tomorrow

好	在	好在
hǎo	**zài**	**hǎozài**
good	be/at/live	fortunately

If you think about it, the same thing happens in English. If you know what "battle" and "ship" mean, you can probably guess what a "battleship" might be. But this wouldn't work with "championship"! Similarly, you'd be unlikely to guess the meaning of "honeymoon" if you only knew the words "honey" and "moon".

The good news is that compound words can help you learn the characters. For example, you may know (from your Chinese lessons) that **xīngqī** means "week". So when you see that this word is written 星期, you will know that 星 is pronounced **xīng**, and 期 is pronounced **qī**—even when these characters are forming part of *other* words. In fact, you will find that you remember some characters *because* they are half of a familiar word.

When you see a word written in characters, you can also often see how the word came to mean what it does. For example, **xīngqī** is 星期 which literally means "star period". This will help you to remember both the word *and* the two individual characters.

What is a stroke-count?
Each Chinese character is made up of a number of pen or brush strokes. Each individual stroke is the mark made by a pen or brush before lifting it off the paper to write the next stroke. Strokes come in various shapes and sizes—a stroke can be a straight line, a curve, a bent line, a line with a hook, or a dot. There is a traditional and very specific way that every character should be drawn. The order *and* direction of the strokes are both important if the character is to have the correct appearance.

What counts as a stroke is determined by tradition and is not always obvious. For example, the small box that often appears as part of a character (like the one on page 32, in the character 名) counts as three strokes, not four! (This is because a single stroke is traditionally used to write the top and right-hand side of the box).

All this may sound rather pedantic but it is well worth learning how to write the characters correctly and with the correct number of strokes. One reason is that knowing how to count the strokes correctly is useful for looking up characters in dictionaries, as you'll see later.

This book shows you how to write characters stroke by stroke, and once you get the feel of it you'll very quickly learn how to work out the stroke-count of a character you haven't met before, *and* get it right!

What are radicals?
Although the earliest characters were simple drawings, most characters are complex with two or more parts. And you'll find that some simple characters appear over and over again as parts of many complex characters. Have a look at these five characters:

她 she		好 good
媽 mother		姓 surname
姐 older sister		

All five of these characters have the same component on the left-hand side: 女, which means "woman". This component gives a clue to the meaning of the character, and is called the "radical". As you can see, most of these five characters have something to do with the idea of "woman", but as you can also see, it's not a totally reliable way of guessing the meaning of the characters. (Meanings of characters are something you just have to learn, without much help from their component parts).

Unfortunately the radical isn't always on the left-hand side of a character. Sometimes it's on the right, or on the top, or on the bottom. Here are some examples:

Character	Radical	Position of radical
都	阝	right
星	日	top
您	心	bottom
這	辶	left and bottom

Because it's not always easy to tell what the radical is for a particular character, it's given explicitly in a separate box for each of the characters in this book. However, as you learn more and more characters, you'll find that you can often guess the radical just by looking at a character.

Why bother with radicals? Well, for hundreds of years Chinese dictionaries have used the radical components of the characters as a way of grouping them. All characters, even the really simple ones, are assigned to one radical or another so that they can be placed within the index of a Chinese dictionary (see the next section).

Incidentally, when you take away the radical, what's left is often a clue to the *pronunciation* of the character (this remainder is called the "phonetic component"). For example, 嗎 and 媽 are formed by adding two different radicals to the character 馬 "horse" and is pronounced **mǎ**. Now 嗎 is pronounced **ma** and 媽 is pronounced **mā**, so you can see that these two characters have inherited their pronunciations from the pronunciation of the phonetic component 馬. Unfortunately these "phonetic components" aren't very dependable either: for example 也 on its own is pronounced **yě** but 他 and 她 are both pronounced **tā**.

How do I find a character in an index or a dictionary?
This is a question lots of people ask, and the answer varies according to the type of dictionary. Many dictionaries today are organized alphabetically by pronunciation. So if you want to look up a character in a dictionary and you know its pronunciation, then it's easy. It's when you don't know the pronunciation of a character that there's a problem, since there is no alphabetical order for characters like there is for English words.

If you don't know the pronunciation of a character, the next best thing is often to use a radical index (which is why radicals are useful). To use this you have to know which part of the character is the radical, and you will also need to be able to count the number of strokes that make up the character. To look up 姓, for example, 女 is the radical (which has 3 strokes) and the remainder 生 has 5 strokes. So first you find the radical 女 amongst

the 3-stroke radicals in the radical index. Then, if there are lots of characters under 女, look for 姓 in the subsection which lists all the characters which have 5-stroke remainders.

This workbook has both a Hanyu Pinyin index and a radical index. Why not get used to how these indexes work by picking a character in the book and seeing if you can find it in both indexes?

Many dictionaries also have a pure stroke-count index (i.e. ignoring the radical). To use this you must count up the strokes in the character as a whole and look the character up under that number (so you would look up– 姓 under 8 strokes). As you can imagine, this type of index can leave you with columns of characters to scan before you find the one you're looking for, so it's usually a last resort!

All these methods have their pitfalls and complications, so recently a completely new way of looking up characters has been devised. The *Chinese Character Fast Finder* (see the inside back cover) organizes characters purely by their shapes so that you can look up any one of 3,000 characters very quickly without knowing its meaning, radical, pronunciation or stroke-count!

How to use this workbook?
One good way to learn characters is to practice writing them, especially if you think about what each character means as you write it. This will fix the characters in your memory better than if you just look at them without writing them.

If you're working on your own without a teacher, work through only a few characters at a time. Go at a pace that suits you; it's much better to do small but regular amounts than to do large chunks at irregular intervals. You might start with just one or two characters each day and increase this as you get better at it. Frequent repetition is the key! Try to get into a daily routine of learning a few new characters and also reviewing the ones you learned on previous days. It's also a good idea to keep a list of which characters you've learned each day, and then to 'test yourself' on the characters you learned the previous day, three days ago, a week ago and a month ago. Each time you test yourself they will stay in your memory for a longer period.

But *don't* worry if you can't remember a character you wrote out ten times only yesterday! This is quite normal to begin with. Just keep going—it will all be sinking in without you realizing it.

Once you've learned a few characters you can use flash cards to test yourself on them in a random order. You can make your own set of cards, or use a ready—made set like *Chinese in a Flash* (see the inside back cover).

How to write characters?

Finally, let's get down to earth and talk about actually writing the characters!

For each character in this book, the first few boxes underneath it show how the character is built up, stroke by stroke. There is a correct way to draw each character, and the diagrams in the boxes show you both the order to draw the strokes in, and also the direction for each stroke.

Use the three gray examples to trace over and then carry on by yourself, drawing the strokes in the correct order and direction. The varying thickness of the lines shows you what the characters would look like if they were drawn with a brush, but if you're using a pencil or ball-point pen don't worry about this. Just trace down the middle of the lines and you will produce good hand-written characters.

Pay attention to the length of each of the strokes so that your finished character has the correct proportions. Use the gray dotted lines inside each box as a guide to help you start and end each stroke in the right place.

You may think that it doesn't really matter how the strokes are written as long as the end result looks the same. To some extent this is true, but there are some good reasons for knowing the "proper" way to write characters. Firstly, it helps you to count strokes, and secondly it will make your character "look right", and also help you to read other people's hand-written characters later on. It's better in the long run to learn the correct method of writing characters from the beginning because, like with so many other things, once you get into 'bad' habits it can be very hard to break them!

If you are left-handed, just use your left hand as normal, but still make sure you use the correct stroke order and direction. For example, draw your horizontal strokes left to right, even if it feels more natural to draw them right to left.

For each Chinese character there is a fixed, correct order in which to write the strokes. But these "stroke-orders" do follow some fairly general rules. The main thing to remember is that:

- you generally work left to right and top to bottom.

Some other useful guidelines are:

- Horizontal lines are written before vertical ones (see 十, page 19);
- Lines that slope down and to the left are written before those that slope down and to the right (see 文, page 41);
- A central part or vertical line is written before symmetrical or smaller lines at the sides (see 小, page 47);
- The top and sides of an outer box are written first, then the interior, then the bottom to "close" it (see 國, page 56).

As you work through the book you'll see these rules in action and get a feel for them, and then you'll know how to draw virtually any Chinese character without having to be shown.

Writing practice

Your first attempts at writing will be awkward, but as with most things you'll get better with practice. That's why there are lots of squares for you to use. And don't be too hard on yourself (we all draw clumsy-looking characters when we start); just give yourself plenty of time and practice. After a while, you'll be able to look back at your early attempts and compare them with your most recent ones, and see just how much you've improved.

After writing the same character a number of times (a row or two at most), try going on to another one. Don't fill up the whole page at one sitting! Then after looking at other characters, come back later and do a few more of the first one. Can you remember the stroke order without having to look at the diagrams?

Finally, try writing out sentences, or just lines of characters, on ordinary paper. To begin with you can mark out squares to write in if you want to, but after that simply imagine the squares and try to keep your characters all equally sized and equally spaced.

Have fun, and remember—the more you do the easier it gets!

	common words	1 stroke

一

yī one; single; a(n)

common words

一個　**yīgè**　a(n); one (of something)
一次　**yīcì**　once
一同／一起　**yītóng/yīqǐ**　together
一月　**yīyuè**　January
十一　**shíyī**　eleven
第一　**dìyī**　first
星期一　**xīngqīyī**　Monday

1 stroke

radical

一

二	common words		2 strokes

common words

二十　**èrshí**　twenty
二妹　**èrmèi**　second younger sister
二月　**èryuè**　February
二手　**èrshǒu**　second hand
十二　**shíèr**　twelve
第二　**dìèr**　second
星期二　**xīngqīèr**　Tuesday

èr two (number)

2 strokes

radical

二

		common words				3 strokes

三

sān three

common words

三十 **sānshí** thirty
三月 **sānyuè** March
三個月 **sāngèyuè** three months
三明治 **sānmíngzhì** sandwich
十三 **shísān** thirteen
第三 **dìsān** third
星期三 **xīngqīsān** Wednesday

3 strokes

radical

一

四

sì four

radical

口

common words

四十　**sìshí**　fourty
四百　**sìbǎi**　four hundred
四月　**sìyuè**　April
四處　**sìchù**　everywhere
十四　**shísì**　fourteen
第四　**dìsì**　fourth
星期四　**xīngqīsì**　Thursday

丨	冂	四	四	四	四	四	四

五

wǔ five

common words

五十　**wǔshí**　fifty
五月　**wǔyuè**　May
五年　**wǔnián**　five years
五本　**wǔběn**　five (books)
十五　**shíwǔ**　fifteen
第五　**dìwǔ**　fifth
星期五　**xīngqīwǔ**　Friday

4 strokes

radical

二

一	丆	五	五	五	五	五

	六				4 strokes
:-:	:--				:-:
	common words				radical
	六十三 **liùshísān** sixty-three				八
	六月 **liùyuè** June				
	六個月 **liùgèyuè** six months				
	六天 **liùtiān** six days				
	十六 **shíliù** sixteen				
liù six	第六 **dìliù** sixth				
	星期六 **xīngqīliù** Saturday				

七

qī seven

		2 strokes
		radical
		一

common words

七十七 **qīshíqī** seventy-seven
七百 **qībǎi** seven hundred
七月 **qīyuè** July
十七 **shíqī** seventeen
七七八八 **qīqībābā** almost complete
七上八下 **qīshàngbāxià** worry; anxious
第七 **dìqī** seventh

一 七 七 七 七

16

| 八 | | common words | | | | 2 strokes | |
| | | | | | | radical 八 | |

bā eight

八十二 **bāshíèr** eighty-two
八百零五 **bābǎilíngwǔ** eight-hundred and five
八月 **bāyuè** August
八成 **bāchéng** 80 per cent
八折 **bāzhé** 20 per cent discount
十八 **shíbā** eighteen
第八 **dìbā** eighth

八	八	八	八	八			

九

jiǔ nine

2 strokes

radical

乙

十

shí ten

common words

十千/一萬 **shíqiān/yīwàn** ten thousand
十月 **shíyuè** October
十一月 **shíyīyuè** November
十二月 **shíèryuè** December
十分 **shífēn** 1. ten points 2. very
十全十美 **shíquánshíměi** perfect; ideal
第十 **dìshí** tenth

2 strokes

radical

十

一　十　十　十　十

你

nǐ you

common words

你好 **nǐ hǎo** How do you do?
你的 **nǐ de** your; yours
你們 **nǐmen** you (plural)
你們的 **nǐmen de** your; yours (plural)

radical

人（亻）

您

nín you (polite)

您好 **nín hǎo** How do you do? (polite)

您早 **nín zǎo** Good morning!

您貴姓? **nín guìxìng** your family name?

11 strokes

radical

心

| 好 | **common words** | **6 strokes** |
| | | **radical** 女 |

hǎo/hào 1. good 2. alright 3. like

好啊! **hǎo a** Good!; OK!
好看 **hǎokàn** 1. good show 2. good looking
好久 **hǎojiǔ** a long time
很好 **hěnhǎo** very good
還好 **háihǎo** still alright
那好 **nà hǎo** alright then ... (agreeing to a suggestion)

		common words		15 strokes	

請

qǐng 1. please
2. to invite

common words

請問 **qǐngwèn** May I ask ...?
請坐 **qǐngzuò** Please sit down.
請進 **qǐngjìn** Please come in.
請客 **qǐngkè** play host; treat
請教 **qǐngjiào** seek advice
請假 **qǐngjià** take leave

15 strokes

radical

言

simplified form

请

問	**common words**	11 strokes
	問好 **wènhǎo** say hello to...	**radical**
	問題 **wèntí** question; problem	口
	問答 **wèndá** question and answer	**simplified form**
wèn ask	學問 **xuéwèn** knowledge	问
	訪問 **fǎngwèn** 1. visit 2. interview	

貴	**common words**	**12 strokes**
	貴姓 **guìxìng** your honorable surname?	**radical**
	貴人 **guìrén** respected person	貝
	貴客/貴賓 **guìkè/guìbīn** distinguished guest; VIP	**simplified form**
guì 1. honorable 2. expensive; valuable	太貴了 **tàiguìle** too expensive 名貴 **mínguì** valuable	贵

1 丶	2 口	3 口	4 中	5 虫	6 虫	7 青	8 青
9 青	10 青	11 貴	12 貴	貴	貴	貴	

姓	**common words** 姓名 **xìngmíng** full name 同姓 **tóngxìng** having the same surname 老百姓 **lǎobǎixìng** common people	**8 strokes** radical 女

xìng surname

姓 姓 姓

	common words	5 strokes
他	他的 **tā de** his 他們 **tāmen** they; them (male) 他們的 **tāmen de** their; theirs (male) 他人／其他人 **tārén/qítārén** other people 其他 **qítā** other	radical 人（亻）
tā he		

亻	亻	亻	亻	他	他	他	他

她	**common words** 她的 **tā de** hers 她們 **tāmen** they; them (female) 她們的 **tāmen de** their; theirs (female)	**6 strokes** **radical** 女
tā she		

1 く	女 2	3 女	如 4	妣 5	她 6	她	她
她							

叫

jiào 1. call; be called
      2. shout 3. order

common words

叫門 **jiàomén** call at the door
叫好 **jiàohǎo** cheer
叫喊 **jiàohǎn** shout; yell
叫做 **jiàozuò** be called
叫車 **jiàochē** order a cab
大叫 **dàjiào** call out loudly

5 strokes

radical

口

丨	口	口	叫	叫	叫	叫	叫

什	**common words**	**4 strokes**
	什麼 **shénme** what	**radical**
	什麼的 **shénme de** etc; so on...	人（亻）
shén/shí 1. mixed	什至 **shénzhì** even to the point that	
2. tenth (mathematics)		

ノ¹	イ²	仁 → ³	什⁴	什	什	什	

麼	**common words**	**14 strokes**
	什麼 **shénme** what	**radical**
	怎麼 **zěnme** how	麻
	那麼 **nàme** in that way; so...	
me interrogative particle	多麼 **duōme** no matter how	**simplified form**
	為什麼？ **wèi shènme** why?	么

名

míng 1. name
2. fame

common words

名字　**míngzi**　name
名叫　**míngjiào**　named
名人　**míngrén**　celebrity; famous person
同名　**tóngmíng**　having the same name
出名　**chūmíng**　become famous; well-known
第一名　**dìyīmíng**　first in position

6 strokes

radical

口

名

字		**common words**			**6 strokes**
		字母 **zìmǔ** letter (alphabet)			**radical**
		字典 **zìdiǎn** dictionary			子
		十字 **shízì** cross			
		漢字 **Hànzì** Chinese (Han) character			
		寫字 **xiězì** write word			
zì written character		生字 **shēngzì** new word			

我

wǒ I; me

common words

我的 **wǒ de** my; mine
我們／咱們 **wǒmen/zánmen** we; us
我國 **wǒguó** our country
我家 **wǒjiā** my family; my home
自我 **zìwǒ** self

7 strokes

radical

戈

是		**9 strokes**

common words

是的 **shì de** yes
是啊 **shì a** yes; yeah
是不是 **shìbùshì** to be or not to be
不是 **bùshì** not to be; no
還是 **háishì** or
老是 **lǎoshì** always

radical

日

shì to be; yes

丨	冂	日	日	旦	早	昆	昰

是	是	是	是			

大		common words				3 strokes
		大聲點 **dàshēngdiǎn** louder				
		大家 **dàjiā** everybody				radical
		大不了 **dàbùliǎo** at the worst				大
		大多／大都／大半 **dàduō/dàdū/dàbàn** mostly				
		大便 **dàbiàn** shit				
dà big; great		大概 **dàgài** probably				
		自大 **zìdà** proud; arrogant				

一	大	大	大	大	大		

學

xué learn

common words

學會 **xuéhuì** learned; mastered
學習 **xuéxí** study
上學 **shàngxué** go to school
放學 **fàngxué** finish school for the day
開學 **kāixué** school reopens
小學 **xiǎoxué** primary school
中學 **zhōngxué** middle/secondary school

16 strokes

radical

子

simplified form

学

學 學 學

生

shēng 1. give birth;
born 2. raw

radical
生

common words

生日　**shēngrì**　birthday
生氣　**shēngqí**　angry
生病　**shēngbìng**　fall sick; not well
生吃　**shēngchī**　eat raw food
學生　**xuésheng**　student
先生　**xiānsheng**　1. Mr 2. husband
醫生　**yīshēng**　doctor

丿　与　与　牛　生　生　生　生

中

zhōng 1. in the middle 2. among 3. (in the) course

common words
中國　**Zhōngguó**　China
中文　**zhōngwén**　Chinese language (written)
中間　**zhōngjiān**　between; in the middle
中年　**zhōngnián**　middle-aged
心中　**xīnzhōng**　in one's heart
手中　**shǒuzhōng**　on hand

4 strokes

radical
丨

英

yīng 1. related to England 2. hero

common words

英國 **Yīngguó** England
英文 **yīngwén** English language (written)
英語 **yīngyǔ** English language
英俊 **yīngjùn** handsome
英明 **yīngmíng** wise
英雄 **yīngxióng** hero

8 strokes

radical

艸 (艹)

一 艹 艹 艹 苎 苹 英 英

英 英 英

文

wén written language; writing

radical

文

common words

文字 **wénzì** script; writing
文具 **wénjù** stationery
文學 **wénxué** literature
語文 **yǔwén** language (spoken and written)
法文 **fǎwén** French (written)
日文 **rìwén** Japanese (written)

課

kè lesson; class

common words

課本　**kèběn**　textbook
課題　**kètí**　topic (of lessons)
課文　**kèwén**　text
上課　**shàngkè**　attend class
下課　**xiàkè**　finish class
功課　**gōngkè**　homework
第一課　**dìyīkè**　first lesson; lesson one

15 strokes

radical

言

simplified form

课

丶 1	二 2	言 3	言 4	言 5	言 6	言 7	訁 8
訁 9	訁 10	誩 11	誩 12	課 13	課 14	課 15	課
課	課						

老

lǎo old

common words

老師　**lǎoshī**　teacher
老大　**lǎodà**　1. eldest sibling 2. gang leader
老婆　**lǎopo**　wife (informal)
老公　**lǎogōng**　husband (informal)
老婆婆　**lǎopópo**　old woman
老外　**lǎowài**　foreigner
古老　**gǔlǎo**　ancient

6 strokes

radical

老

一 十 土 耂 耂 老 老 老

老

師

shī teacher; master

common words

師生 **shīshēng** teacher and student
師父 **shīfu** master
老師／教師 **lǎoshī/jiàoshī** teacher
律師 **lùshī** lawyer
廚師 **chúshī** chef

10 strokes

radical

巾

simplified form

师

⺁¹	亻²	³⺁	自⁴	自⁵	自⁶	師⁷	師⁸
師⁹	師¹⁰	師	師	師			

同

tóng the same; together

common words

同學 **tóngxué** classmate
同班 **tóngbān** same class
同時 **tóngshí** same time
同樣 **tóngyàng** the same; alike
同事 **tóngshì** colleague
一同／一起 **yītóng/yīqǐ** together

6 strokes

radical

口

校

xiào school

common words

校長 **xiàozhǎng** principal
校服 **xiàofú** school uniform
校友 **xiàoyǒu** schoolmate; alum
學校 **xuéxiào** school
同校 **tóngxiào** same school
上校 **shàngxiào** colonel

10 strokes

radical

木

一	十	才	木	朮	杧	杧	杧

杧	校	校	校	校			

小

xiǎo small; little

common words

小姐　**xiǎojiě**　Miss; lady
小時　**xiǎoshí**　hour
小時候　**xiǎoshíhòu**　childhood
小心　**xiǎoxīn**　(be) careful
小看　**xiǎokàn**　belittle; underestimate
小便　**xiǎobiàn**　urine; urinate

3 strokes

radical

小

小　小　小　小　小　小

朋	**common words**	8 strokes
	朋友　**péngyǒu**　friend	radical
	好朋友　**hǎopéngyǒu**　good friend	月
	男朋友　**nánpéngyǒu**　boyfriend	
	女朋友　**nǚpéngyǒu**　girlfriend	
péng friend	老朋友　**lǎopéngyǒu**　old friend	
	小朋友　**xiǎopéngyǒu**　kid; child	

丿	月	月	月	刖	朋	朋	朋
朋	朋	朋					

友		**common words**			4 strokes	
		友人 **yǒurén** friend			radical	
		友誼／友情 **yǒuyì/yǒuqíng** friendship			又	
		好友 **hǎoyǒu** good friend				
		男友 **nányǒu** boyfriend				
		女友 **nǚyǒu** girlfriend				
yǒu friend		工友 **gōngyǒu** fellow worker; caretaker				

一	𠂇	方	友	友	友	友

們	common words	10 strokes
men plural suffix (for persons)	你們 **nǐmen** you (plural) 我們／咱們 **wǒmen/zánmen** we; us 女士們 **nǚshìmen** ladies 男士們 **nánshìmen** gentlemen 同學們 **tóngxuémen** classmates 人們 **rénmen** people	radical 人（亻） simplified form 们

亻1	亻2	們3	們4	們5	們6	們7	們8
們9	們10	們	們	們			

呢

ne question particle

common words

你呢？ **nǐ ne** How about you?
他（她）呢？ **tā ne** How about him (her)?
我們呢？ **wǒmen ne** How about us?
人呢？ **rén ne** Where's the person?

8 strokes

radical

口

	common words					**17 strokes**
謝	謝謝 **xièxie** thank you					**radical** 言
	謝詞 **xiècí** thank you speech					
	多謝 **duōxiè** many thanks					**simplified form**
	不謝 **bùxiè** don't mention it					
xiè thank	答謝 **dáxiè** express appreciation					谢

1 丶	2 二	3 言	4 言	5 言	6 言	7 言	8 言
9 訂	10 訂	11 詞	12 詞	13 諍	14 諍	15 謝	16 謝
17 謝	謝	謝	謝				

再	**common words**	6 strokes
	再見/再會 **zàijiàn/zàihuì** Goodbye!	**radical**
zài again	再三 **zàisān** again and again; repeatedly	冂
	再次 **zàicì** once more	
	再不 **zàibù** or; or else	
	一再 **yīzài** again and again; repeatedly	
	不再 **bùzài** no longer; never again	

見

jiàn see; meet

common words

見好 **jiànhǎo** get better (from an illness)
見面 **jiànmiàn** meet
不見了 **bùjiànle** missing; can't be found
不見得 **bùjiànde** not necessarily
看見 **kànjiàn** see
少見 **shǎojiàn** rare
聽見 **tīngjiàn** hear

7 strokes

radical

見

simplified form

见

丨	冂	月	目	目	貝	見	見
見	見						

54

美

měi beautiful

common words	**9 strokes**
美麗 **měilì** beautiful; pretty	
美好 **měihǎo** wonderful	**radical**
美食 **měishí** delicacy	羊 （⺷）
美女／美人 **měinǚ/měirén** beautiful girl/woman	
美國 **Měiguó** (the) Unites States of America	
很美／太美了 **hěnměi/tàiměile** very beautiful	

55

國		common words		11 strokes

common words

國家 **guójiā** country
國人 **guórén** people in a country
國王 **guówáng** king
出國 **chūguó** go abroad
外國 **wàiguó** foreign country
外國人 **wàiguórén** people from other country

guó country; national

11 strokes

radical

口

simplified form

国

1	2	3	4	5	6	7	8

9	10	11	國	國	國		

		common words		2 strokes		

人

rén person; people

common words

人人/每人 **rénrén/měirén** everyone
人口 **rénkǒu** population
工人 **gōngrén** worker
大人/成人 **dàrén/chéngrén** adult
本人 **běnrén** oneself
客人 **kèrén** guest

2 strokes

radical

人（亻）

ノ¹	人²	人	人	人			

嗎	**common words**	**13 strokes**
	是嗎? **shìma** Is that so?; Is it?	**radical**
	好嗎? **hǎoma** good?; alright?	口
	忙嗎? **mángma** busy?	
	行嗎? **xíngma** Is it okay?	**simplified form**
	可以嗎? **kěyǐma** May I?	
ma question particle	有事嗎? **yǒushìma** what's up?	吗

| 丨 | 口 | 口 | 口 | 口 | 口 | 口 | 口 |
| 1 | 2 | 3 | 口 4 | 口 5 | 口 6 | 口 7 | 口 8 |

| 嗎 | 嗎 | 嗎 | 嗎 | 嗎 | 嗎 | 嗎 | 嗎 |
| 9 | 10 | 11 | 12 | 13 | | | |

也

yě also; too

common words

也是 **yěshì** is also ...
也好 **yěhǎo** may as well
也許 **yěxǔ** perhaps

3 strokes

radical

乙

フ	也	也	也	也	也		

不

bù not; no

common words

不對 **bùduì** wrong; incorrect

不要 **bùyào** don't want

不會 **bùhuì** don't know

不同/不一樣 **bùtóng/bùyīyàng** it's different

不客氣 **bùkèqi** not at all; don't mention it

不好意思 **bùhǎoyìsi** 1. embarrassed 2. excuse me

對不起 **duìbuqǐ** sorry

一	丁	不	不	不	不	不	

	common words					15 strokes	
誰	誰的 **shéi de/shuí de** whose					radical 言	
shéi/shuí who	誰知道 **shéi zhīdào/shuí zhīdào** no one knows					simplified form 谁	

⟍¹	²⁼	³⁼	⁴⁼	⁼⁵	言⁶	言⁷	訐⁸
訐⁹	訐¹⁰	訐¹¹	誰¹²	誰¹³	誰¹⁴	誰¹⁵	誰
誰	誰						

的

de particle

common words

我的 **wǒ de** my; mine
你的 **nǐ de** your; yours
他的/她的 **tā de** his/hers
誰的 **shéi de/shuí de** whose
有的 **yǒude** some
挺好的 **tǐnghǎo de** quite good

8 strokes

radical

白

家		**common words** 家庭 **jiātíng** family 家人 **jiārén** family member 人家 **rénjiā** other people 回家 **huíjiā** return home 每家/家家 **měijiā/jiājiā** every family; every household 一家大小 **yījiādàxiǎo** everyone in a family		**10 strokes** radical 宀	
jiā family; home					

爸		common words		8 strokes
		爸爸 **bàba** father 爸爸媽媽 **bàbamāma** parents 老爸 **lǎobà** father		radical 父
bà father				

⺍¹	⺍²	少³	⁴父	爷⁵	爸⁶	爸⁷	爸⁸
爸	爸	爸					

和

hé 1. ...and...
2. harmony

common words

和好 **héhǎo** reconcile
和氣 **héqì** amiable; friendly
和平 **hépíng** peace
和事老 **héshìlǎo** mediator

8 strokes

radical

口

和 和 和

媽

mā mother

common words

媽媽 **māma** mother
姨媽 **yímā** aunt (mother's married sister)
姑媽 **gūmā** aunt (father's married sister)

13 strokes

radical
女

simplified form

妈

哥

gē older brother

common words

哥哥 **gēge** older brother
大哥 **dàgē** eldest brother
二哥 **èrgē** second elder brother
哥兒們 **gērmen** 1. brothers 2. buddies
帥哥 **shuàigē** handsome man

姐

jiě older sister

common words

姐姐 **jiějie** older sister
姐妹 **jiěmèi** sisters
大姐 **dàjiě** 1. eldest sister 2. older woman
二姐 **èrjiě** second elder sister
小姐 **xiǎojiě** Miss; lady
空姐 **kōngjiě** air stewardess

8 strokes

radical

女

⟨	女	女	如	如	姐	姐	姐
姐	姐	姐					

弟

dì younger brother

common words

弟弟　**dìdi**　younger brother
弟妹　**dìmèi**　younger brother and sister
兄弟　**xiōngdì**　brothers
姐弟　**jiědì**　older sister and younger brother
徒弟　**túdì**　disciple; follower

7 strokes

radical

弓

妹

mèi younger sister

common words

妹妹 **mèimei** younger sister
大妹 **dàmèi** first younger sister
三妹 **sānmèi** third younger sister
小妹 **xiǎomèi** youngest sister
姐妹 **jiěmèi** sisters
兄弟姐妹 **xiōngdìjiěmèi** brothers and sisters

8 strokes

radical

女

住

zhù 1. live; stay
        2. stop

common words

住家 **zhùjiā** residence
住址 **zhùzhǐ** address
住口 **zhùkǒu** shut up
住手 **zhùshǒu** Hands off!
站住 **zhànzhù** Halt!
記住 **jìzhù** remember

亻	亻	亻	亻	仁	住	住	住
住	住						

		6 strokes
	common words	radical
在	在嗎? **zàima** in?	土
	在家裡 **zàijiālǐ** at home	
	不在 **bùzài** not in	
	現在 **xiànzài** now; currently	
zài 1. be; at 2. live	還在 **háizài** still there	
	好在 **hǎozài** fortunately	

		common words				10 strokes	

這

zhè this

common words

這兒／這裡 **zhèr/zhèlǐ** here
這些 **zhèxiē** these
這樣 **zhèyàng** this way; like this
這麼 **zhème** such, so
這次 **zhècì** this time
到這兒來 **dàozhèrlái** Come here!

10 strokes

radical
辵（辶）

simplified form

这

女

nǚ female

3 strokes

radical

女

common words

女兒 **nǚér** daughter
女生 **nǚshēng** female student; school girl
女性 **nǚxìng** female gender
女士 **nǚshì** Madam
女人 **nǚrén** 1. wife 2. mistress
婦女 **fùnǚ** woman

兒

ér/r 1. child 2. suffix

radical

儿

simplified form

儿

common words

兒子 **érzi** son
兒童 **értóng** child
大兒子 **dàérzi** eldest son
小兒子 **xiǎoérzi** youngest son
一會兒 **yīhuìr** a moment; a short while
一點兒 **yīdiǎnr** a little

兒 兒 兒

那

nà/nèi 1. that
2. in that case

common words

那個 **nàge** that
那裡／那兒 **nàlǐ/nàr** there
那麼 **nàme** in that case; then
那麼點兒 **nàmediǎnr** such small amount ...
那些 **nàxiē** those

6 strokes

radical

邑（右阝）

男

nán male

common words	

男孩/男孩子 **nánhái/nánháizi** boy
男生 **nánshēng** male student; school boy
男人 **nánrén** man
男性 **nánxìng** male gender
男男女女 **nánnán-nǚnǚ** boys and girls
男厕/男厕所 **náncè/náncèsuǒ** man's toilet

7 strokes
radical
田

丨¹	口²	曰³	甲⁴	田⁵	甼⁶	男⁷	男
男	男						

孩	**common words**	**9 strokes**
	孩子/小孩 **háizi/xiǎohái** child	**radical**
	孩子氣 **háiziqì** childish	子
hái child	孩子話 **háizihuà** childish words	
	男孩/男孩子 **nánhái/nánháizi** boy	
	女孩/女孩子 **nǚhái/nǚháizi** girl	

子

zi/zǐ 1. son 2. seed
3. suffix (noun)

common words

子女/兒女 **zǐnǚ/érnǚ** son and daughter; children
兒子 **érzi** son
妻子 **qīzi** wife
桌子 **zhuōzi** table; desk
車子 **chēzi** 1. vehicle (small scale) 2. bicycle
一下子 **yīxiàzi** 1. all of a sudden 2. all at once

3 strokes

radical

子

都

dōu/dū 1. all; even
2. big city

common words

都有 **dōuyǒu** all have
都是 **dōushì** all are
都會 **dōuhuì** all know how to do
都市／都會 **dūshì/dūhuì** big city
首都 **shǒudū** capital city

10 strokes

radical

邑（右 阝）

一	十	土	耂	者	者	者
都	都	都	都	都		

沒

méi haven't; without

common words

沒有　**méiyǒu**　don't have; haven't
沒錯　**méicuò**　correct
沒問題　**méi wèntí**　no question; no problem
沒事　**méishì**　1. free 2. no problem; alright
沒關係/沒什麼　**méiguānxi/méishénme**
it doesn't matter
還沒　**háiméi**　not yet

7 strokes

radical

水（氵）

simplified form

没

丶	冫	氵	氵	沪	沒	沒	沒
沒	沒						

有

yǒu has; have

common words

有的/有些 **yǒude/yǒuxiē** some
有學問 **yǒu xuéwèn** knowledgeable
有點兒 **yǒudiǎnr** a little; somewhat
有沒有(?) **yǒu méiyǒu** 1. did you? 2. whether or not
祇有 **zhǐyǒu** there's only ...
還有 **háiyǒu** moreover; furthermore

一　ナ　ナ　有　有　有　有

有

做	**common words**	**11 strokes**
	做好/做完 **zuòhǎo/zuòwán** finish; complete	**radical**
	做錯 **zuòcuò** do wrongly	人（亻）
zuò do; make	做人 **zuòrén** be an upright person	

做飯 **zuòfàn** cook a meal

做作業 **zuò zuòyè** do assignment

做工 **zuògōng** work

	common words	8 strokes
事	事事/每事 **shìshì/měishì** every matter 事前 **shìqián** in advance; beforehand 事後 **shìhòu** afterwards; after the event 小事 **xiǎoshì** trivial matter 故事 **gùshì** story 做事 **zuòshì** 1. work 2. deal with matters	radical 亅

shì matter

兩

liǎng two

common words

兩個月 **liǎnggèyuè** two months
兩百 **liǎngbǎi** two hundred
兩次 **liǎngcì** twice
兩樣 **liǎngyàng** two types; different
兩口子 **liǎngkǒuzi** a couple; husband and wife
沒兩樣 **méi liǎngyàng** the same

8 strokes

radical

入

simplified form

两

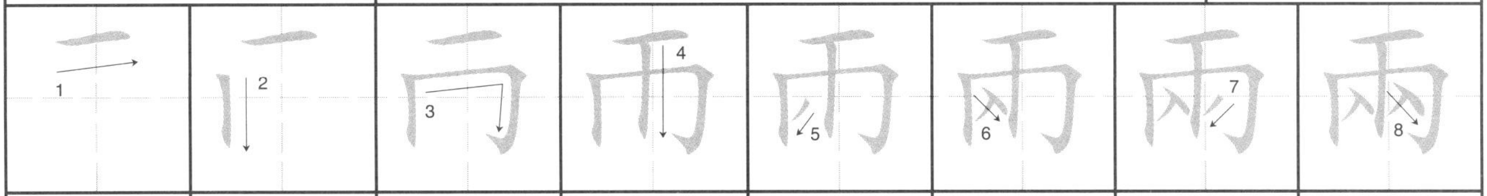

兩 兩 兩

個

gè most common
measure word

common words

個個/每個 **gègè/měigè** each one (of something)
個人 **gèrén** individual
個子 **gèzi** body size
兩個門 **liǎnggèmén** two doors
那個 **nàge** that
這個 **zhège** this; this one

10 strokes

radical

人（亻）

simplified form

个

多

duō 1. many, much
2. far more

common words

多少(?) **duōshǎo** 1. how many/much? 2. tend to
多大(?) **duōdà** 1. how old(?) 2. how big(?)
多半 **duōbàn** more often than not
多麼 **duōme** no matter how
差不多 **chābùduō** about; more or less

6 strokes

radical

夕

少	common words	4 strokes
	少女　**shàonǚ**　teenage girl	
	少不了　**shǎobuliǎo**　can't do without	radical
	青少年　**qīngshàonián**　teenager	小
	很少　**hěnshǎo**　very little; very few	
shǎo/shào　1. few; little 2. young	不少　**bùshǎo**　quite a lot	
	男女老少　**nánnǚlǎoshào**　young and old	

丨	丨	小	少	少	少	少	

時

shí time

common words	10 strokes
時間 **shíjiān** time	**radical** 日
時期 **shíqī** period of time	
時時／不時 **shíshí/bùshí** often	**simplified form**
一時 **yīshí** temporarily; momentarily	
有時／有時候 **yǒushí/yǒu shíhòu** sometimes	时
到時 **dàoshí** when the time comes	

丨¹	刀²	日³	日⁴	旷⁵	旷⁶	旷⁷	旷⁸
時⁹	時¹⁰	時	時				

間

jiān 1. between
2. room 3. measure word

common words

時間 **shíjiān** time
中間 **zhōngjiān** between; in the middle
房間 **fángjiān** room
夜間 **yèjiān** at night; night time
洗手間 **xǐshǒujiān** washroom
一間客房 **yījiānkèfáng** a guest room

12 strokes

radical

門

simplified form

间

丨	冂	尸	月	門	門	門	門
門	間	間	間	間	間	間	

今

jīn now; at present

4 strokes

radical

人（亻）

common words

今天／今日 **jīntiān/jīnrì** today
今早 **jīnzǎo** this morning
今晚 **jīnwǎn** tonight; this evening
今年 **jīnnián** this year
今後 **jīnhòu** from now on
至今 **zhìjīn** up to now; so far
如今 **rújīn** now; nowadays

ノ	人	仒	今	今	今	今	

天	common words	4 strokes
	天天/每天 **tiāntiān/měitiān** every day	radical
	天上/天空中 **tiānshàng/tiānkōngzhōng** in the sky	大
	天氣 **tiānqì** weather	
	今天 **jīntiān** today	
	明天 **míngtiān** tomorrow	
	昨天 **zuótiān** yesterday	
tiān 1. day 2. sky	白天 **báitiān** daytime	

幾	**common words**	**12 strokes**
	幾個(?) **jǐgè** 1. how many? 2. several (of something)	**radical**
jǐ 1. how many 2. several	幾次(?) **jǐcì** 1. how many times? 2. several times	幺
	幾時(?) **jǐshí** 1. when? 2. anytime	
	幾天(?) **jǐtiān** 1. how many days? 2. several days	**simplified form**
	幾分(?) **jǐfēn** 1. how many points? 2. somewhat	几
	幾點(?) **jǐdiǎn** 1. what time? 2. several dots	

號

hào 1. date 2. size
3. sequence 4. signal

common words

號碼 **hàomǎ** number
幾號? **jǐhào** which number?; what size?; what date?
十號 **shíhào** number ten; size ten; tenth (of a month)
句號 **jùhào** full-stop
逗號 **dòuhào** comma
問號 **wènhào** question mark

13 strokes

radical
虍

simplified form

号

丨	口	口	吕	号	号	号	号
号	号	號	號	號	號	號	號

明

míng bright

common words

明明　**míngmíng**　obviously
明白　**míngbai**　understand
明天/明日　**míngtiān/míngrì**　tomorrow
明亮　**míngliàng**　bright
文明　**wénmíng**　civilized; civilization
發明　**fāmíng**　invent

丨	刀	日	日	明	明	明	明
明	明	明					

年	**common words**
	年年/每年 **niánnián/měinián** every year
	年紀 **niánjì** age
	明年 **míngnián** next year
	後年 **hòunián** year after next year
	去年 **qùnián** last year
nián year	前年 **qiánnián** year before last year

6 strokes

radical

干

ノ¹	仁²	乍³	乍⁴	乍⁵	年⁶	年	年
年							

月		**common words**				**4 strokes**	
		月亮/月球 **yuèliàng/yuèqiú** moon					
		月光 **yuèguāng** moonlight				**radical**	
		這個月 **zhège yuè** this month				月	
		上個月 **shàngge yuè** last month					
yuè 1. month 2. moon		下個月 **xiàge yuè** next month					

刀	刀	月	月	月	月	月	

97

				4 strokes
日	**common words**			
	日本 **Rìběn** Japan			radical
	日期 **rìqī** date			日
	日子 **rìzi** 1. date; day 2. time 3. life			
	今日 **jīnrì** today			
	明日 **míngrì** tomorrow			
rì day	昨日 **zuórì** yesterday			
	每日 **měirì** every day			

丨	冂	日	日	日	日	日	

星

xīng star

common words

星星　**xīngxing**　star
星期　**xīngqī**　week
星座　**xīngzuò**　1. constellation 2. sign of zodiac
星球　**xīngqiú**　heavenly body; planet
歌星　**gēxīng**　singer
明星　**míngxīng**　star (celebrity)

9 strokes

radical

日

星 星 星 星

| | | common words | | | | 12 strokes |
| | | | | | | radical |

期

qī period

common words

期間/時期 **qījiān/shíqī** period of time
學期 **xuéqī** school term; semester
假期 **jiàqī** holiday
到期 **dàoqī** expire
早期 **zǎoqī** earlier time; early stage
上星期 **shàngxīngqī** last week
下星期 **xiàxīngqī** next week

12 strokes

radical

月

		common words			6 strokes

早

zǎo early; morning; Good morning!

common words

早安 **zǎo'ān** Good morning!
早上 **zǎoshang** morning
早日 **zǎorì** (at an) early date; soon
早晚 **zǎowǎn** 1. day and night 2. sooner or later
早饭／早點／早餐 **zǎofàn/zǎodiǎn/zǎocān** breakfast
一早 **yīzǎo** early in the morning
明早 **míngzǎo** tomorrow morning

6 strokes

radical

日

上

shàng 1. above; go up
2. attend 3. previous

common words

上面 **shàngmian** above; top
上來 **shànglái** come up
上去 **shàngqù** go up
上班 **shàngbān** go to work
上廁所 **shàngcèsuǒ** go to the toilet
上次 **shàngcì** last time
馬上 **mǎshàng** immediately

3 strokes

radical

一

上 上 上 上 上

| | common words | | 3 strokes |
| | | | radical 一 |

下

xià 1. under; go down
2. finish 3. next

common words

下面 **xiàmian** underneath; below
下來 **xiàlái** come down
下去 **xiàqù** go down
下班 **xiàbān** finish work
下雨 **xiàyǔ** rain
下次 **xiàcì** next time
一下 **yīxià** 1. one time 2. a short while

午

wǔ noon

common words

午饭/午餐 **wǔfàn/wǔcān** lunch
午覺/午睡 **wǔjiào/wǔshuì** afternoon nap
午夜 **wǔyè** midnight
上午/午前 **shàngwǔ/wǔqián** morning (a.m.)
中午 **zhōngwǔ** noon
下午/午後 **xiàwǔ/wǔhòu** afternoon (p.m.)

4 strokes

radical

十

吃

chī eat

common words

吃饭 **chīfàn** have a meal
吃饱了 **chībǎole** eaten; eaten enough
吃不饱 **chībùbǎo** not full; not enough to eat
吃不下 **chībùxià** not able to eat; have no appetite
小吃 **xiǎochī** snack
好吃 **hǎochī** tasty; delicious

6 strokes

radical
口

晚

wǎn night; late

common words

晚上 **wǎnshang** evening; night
晚安 **wǎn'ān** Good night!
晚飯／晚餐 **wǎnfàn/wǎncān** dinner
晚班 **wǎnbān** evening shift; night shift
晚點 **wǎndiǎn** be late
起晚了 **qǐwǎnle** got up late

12 strokes

radical

日

飯

fàn meal; cooked rice

common words

飯前 **fànqián** before a meal
飯後 **fànhòu** after a meal
飯菜 **fàncài** rice and dishes
飯店 **fàndiàn** 1. restaurant 2. hotel
白飯 **báifàn** cooked white rice
開飯 **kāifàn** start serving a meal

12 strokes

radical

食

simplified form

饭

	common words		2 strokes

了不起 **liǎobuqǐ** fantastic; amazing
對了 **duìle** That's right!
算了 **suànle** forget it
都上學了 **dōushàngxuéle** all have gone to school
受不了 **shòubuliǎo** unbearable
吃了 **chīle** had eaten

le/liǎo particle

radical
乛

哪

nǎ/něi which; any

radical
口

common words

哪個(?) **nǎge** 1. which? 2. any; anyone
哪裡?/哪兒? **nǎlǐ/nǎr** where?
哪樣(?) **nǎyàng** 1. what kind? 2. whatever
哪天(?) **nǎtiān** 1. which day? 2. anyday; someday
哪怕 **nǎpà** no matter

丨	口	口	叮	叼	叼	叼	哪
哪	哪	哪	哪				

Hanyu Pinyin Index

Radical Index

1 stroke

[一]

一	yī	10
七	qī	16
三	sān	12
上	shàng	102
下	xià	103
不	bù	60

[丨]

中	zhōng	39

[乙]

九	jiǔ	18
也	yě	59

[丿]

了	le/liǎo	108
事	shì	84

2 strokes

[二]

二	èr	11
五	wǔ	14

人 [亻]

人	rén	57
今	jīn	91
什	shén/shí	30
他	tā	27
你	nǐ	20
住	zhù	71
們	men	50
個	gè	86
做	zuò	83

[儿]

兒	ér/r	75

[入]

兩	liǎng	85

[八]

八	bā	17
六	liù	15

[冂]

再	zài	53

[十]

十	shí	19
午	wǔ	104

[又]

友	yǒu	49

3 strokes

[口]

叫	jiào	29
同	tóng	45
名	míng	32
吃	chī	105
和	hé	65
呢	ne	51
問	wèn	24
哥	gē	67
哪	nǎ/něi	109
嗎	ma	58

[囗]

四	sì	13
國	guó	56

[土]

在	zài	72

[夕]

多	duō	87

[大]

大	dà	36
天	tiān	92

[女]

女	nǚ	74
好	hǎo/háo	22
她	tā	28
姓	xìng	26
妹	mèi	70
姐	jiě	68
媽	mā	66

[子]

子	zi/zǐ	79
字	zì	33
孩	hái	78
學	xué	37

[宀]

家	jiā	63

[小]

小	xiǎo	47
少	shǎo/shào	88

[巾]

師	shī	44

[干]

年	nián	96

[幺]

幾	jǐ	93

[弓]

弟	dì	69

4 strokes

[心]
您 nín 21

[戈]
我 wǒ 34

[文]
文 wén 41

[日]
日 rì 98
早 zǎo 101
明 míng 95
是 shì 35
星 xīng 99
時 shí 89
晚 wǎn 106

[月]
月 yuè 97
有 yǒu 82
朋 péng 48
期 qī 100

[木]
校 xiào 46

水 [氵]
沒 méi 81

[父]
爸 bà 64

5 strokes

[生]
生 shēng 38

[田]
男 nán 77

[白]
的 de 62

6 strokes

羊 [䒑]
美 měi 55

老
老 lǎo 43

艸 [艹]
英 yīng 40

[虍]
號 hào 94

7 strokes

[見]
見 jiàn 54

[言]
誰 shéi/shuí 61
請 qǐng 23
課 kè 42
謝 xiè 52

[貝]
貴 guì 25

辵 [辶]
這 zhè 73

邑 [右阝]
那 nà/nèi 76
都 dōu/dū 80

8 strokes

[門]
間 jiān 90

9 strokes

[食]
飯 fàn 107

11 strokes

[麻]
麼 me 31

English–Chinese Index

A

a(n) 一 yī *10*

a(n) (of something) 一個 yīgè *10*

a couple 兩口子 liǎngkǒuzi *85*

a guest room 一間客房 yījiānkèfáng *90*

a little 一點兒 yīdiǎnr *75*; 有點兒 yǒudiǎnr *82*

a long time 好久 hǎojiǔ *22*

a moment 一會兒 yīhuìr *75*

a short while 一會兒 yīhuìr *75*; 一下 yīxià *103*

about 差不多 chābùduō *87*

above 上/上面 shàng/shàngmian *102*

address 住址 zhùzhǐ *71*

adult 大人/成人 dàrén/chéngrén *57*

after a meal 飯後 fànhòu *107*

afternoon (p.m.) 下午/午後 xiàwǔ/wǔhòu *104*

afternoon nap 午覺/午睡 wǔjiào/wǔshuì *104*

afterwards/after the event 事後 shìhòu *84*

again 再 zài *53*

again and again 再三/一再 zàisān/yīzài *53*

age 年紀 niánjì *96*

air stewardess 空姐 kōngjiě *68*

alike 同樣 tóngyàng *45*

all 都 dōu *80*

all are 都是 dōushì *80*

all at once 一下子 yīxiàzi *79*

all have 都有 dōuyǒu *80*

all have gone to school 都上學了 dōushàngxuéle *108*

all know how to do 都會 dōuhuì *80*

all of a sudden 一下子 yīxiàzi *79*

almost complete 七七八八 qīqībābā *16*

alright 好 hǎo *22*; 沒事 méishì *81*

alright? 好嗎? hǎoma *58*

alright then ... 那好 nà hǎo *22*

alum 校友 xiàoyǒu *46*

also 也 yě *59*

always 老是 lǎoshì *35*

...and... 和 hé *65*

amazing 了不起 liǎobuqǐ *108*

amiable 和氣 héqì *65*

among 中 zhōng *39*

B

be 在 zài *72*

be an upright person 做人 zuòrén *83*

be called 叫/叫做 jiào/jiàozuò *29*

be late 晚點 wǎndiǎn *106*

beautiful 美/美麗 měi/měilì *55*

beautiful girl 美女 měinǚ *55*

beautiful woman 美人 měirén *55*

become famous 出名 chūmíng *32*

before a meal 飯前 fànqián *107*

beforehand 事前 shìqián *84*

belittle 小看 xiǎokàn *47*

below 下面 xiàmian *103*

between 間/中間 jiān/zhōngjiān *39, 90*

bicycle 車子 chēzi *79*

big 大 dà *36*

big city 都市/都會 dūshì/dūhuì *80*

birthday 生日 shēngrì *38*

body size 個子 gèzi *86*

ancient 古老 gǔlǎo *43*

angry 生氣 shēngqí *38*

anxious 七上八下 qīshàngbāxià *16*

any 哪/哪個 nǎ/nǎge *109*

anyday 哪天 nǎtiān *109*

anyone 哪個 nǎge *109*

anytime 幾時 jǐshí *93*

April 四月 sìyuè *13*

arrogant 自大 zìdà *36*

ask 問 wèn *24*

at 在 zài *72*

at home 在家裡 zàijiālǐ *72*

at night 夜間 yèjiān *90*

at present 今 jīn *91*

at the worst 大不了 dàbùliǎo *36*

attend 上 shàng *102*

attend class 上課 shàngkè *42*

August 八月 bāyuè *17*

aunt (father's married sister) 姑媽 gūmā *66*

aunt (mother's married sister) 姨媽 yímā *66*

E

each one 個個/每個 gègè/měigè 86

early 早 zǎo 101

early date 早日 zǎorì 101

early in the morning 一早 yīzǎo 101

earlier time/early stage 早期 zǎoqī 100

eat 吃 chī 105

eat raw food 生吃 shēngchī 38

eaten/eaten enough 吃飽了 chībǎole 105

eight 八 bā 17

eight-hundred and five 八百零五 bābǎilíngwǔ 17

eighteen 十八 shíbā 17

eighth 第八 dìbā 17

80 per cent 八成 bāchéng 17

eighty-two 八十二 bāshíèr 17

eldest brother 大哥 dàgē 67

eldest sibling 老大 lǎodà 43

eldest sister 大姐 dàjiě 68

eldest son 大兒子 dàérzi 75

eleven 十一 shíyī 10

embarassed 不好意思 bùhǎoyìsi 60

England 英國 Yīngguó 40

English language 英語 yīngyǔ 40

English language (written) 英文 yīngwén 40

etc 什麼的 shénme de 30

even 都 dōu 80

even to the point that 什至 shénzhì 30

evening 晚上 wǎnshang 106

evening shift 晚班 wǎnbān 106

every day 天天/每天 tiāntiān/měitiān 92; 每日 měirì 98

every family 每家/家家 měijiā/jiājiā 63

every matter 事事/每事 shìshì/měishì 84

every year 年年/每年 niánnián/měinián 96

everybody 大家 dàjiā 36

everyone 人人/每人 rénrén/měirén 57

everyone in a family 一家大小 yījiādàxiǎo 63

everywhere 四處 sìchù 13

excuse me 不好意思 bùhǎoyìsi 60

expensive 貴 guì 25

expire 到期 dàoqī 100

express appreciation 答謝 dáxiè 52

F

fall sick 生病 shēngbìng 38

fame 名 míng 32

family 家/家庭 jiā/jiātíng 63

family member 家人 jiārén 63

famous person 名人 míngrén 32

fantastic 了不起 liǎobuqǐ 108

father 爸/爸爸/老爸 bà/bàba/lǎobà 64

far more 多 duō 87

February 二月 èryuè 11

fellow worker 工友 gōngyǒu 49

female 女 nǚ 74

female gender 女性 nǚxìng 74

female student 女生 nǚshēng 74

few 少 shǎo 88

fifteen 十五 shíwǔ 14

fifth 第五 dìwǔ 14

fifty 五十 wǔshí 14

finish (attending) 下 xià 103

finish (doing) 做好/做完 zuòhǎo/zuòwán 83

finish class 下課 xiàkè 42

finish school for the day 放學 fàngxué 37

finish work 下班 xiàbān 103

first 第一 dìyī 10

first in position 第一名 dìyīmíng 32

first lesson 第一課 dìyīkè 42

first younger sister 大妹 dàmèi 70

five 五 wǔ 14

five (books) 五本 wǔběn 14

five years 五年 wǔnián 14

follower 徒弟 túdì 69

foreign country 外國 wàiguó 56

foreigner 老外 lǎowài 43

forget it 算了 suànle 108

fortunately 好在 hǎozài 72

four 四 sì 13

four hundred 四百 sìbǎi 13

fourteen 十四 shísì 13

fourth 第四 dìsì 13

fourty 四十 sìshí 13

free 沒事 méishì 81

French (written) 法文 fǎwén 41

friend 朋友 péngyǒu 48; 友人 yǒurén 49

mediator 和事老 héshìlǎo *65*
meet 見/見面 jiàn/jiànmiàn *54*
middle 中 zhōng *39*
middle school 中學 zhōngxué *37*
middle-aged 中年 zhōngnián *39*
midnight 午夜 wǔyè *104*
mine 我的 wǒ de *34, 62*
Miss 小姐 xiǎojiě *47, 68*
missing 不見了 bùjiànle *54*
mistress 女人 nǚrén *74*
mixed 什 shí *30*
momentarily 一時 yīshí *89*
Monday 星期一 xīngqīyī *10*
month 月 yuè *97*
moon 月/月亮/月球 yuè/yuèliàng/yuèqiú *97*
moonlight 月光 yuèguāng *97*
more often than not 多半 duōbàn *87*
more or less 差不多 chābùduō *87*
moreover 還有 háiyǒu *82*
morning (a.m.) 早/早上 zǎo/zǎoshang *101*; 上午/午前 shàngwǔ/wǔqián *104*
mostly 大多/大都/大半 dàduō/dàdū/dàbàn *36*
mother 媽/媽媽 mā/māma *66*
Mr 先生 xiānsheng *38*
my 我的 wǒ de *34, 62*
my family 我家 wǒjiā *34*
my home 我家 wǒjiā *34*

N
name 名/名字 míng/míngzi *32*
named 名叫 míngjiào *32*
national 國 guó *56*
never again 不再 bùzài *53*
new word 生字 shēngzì *33*
next 下 xià *103*
next month 下個月 xiàge yuè *97*
next time 下次 xiàcì *103*
next week 下星期 xiàxīngqī *100*
next year 明年 míngnián *96*
night shift 晚班 wǎnbān *106*
night 晚/晚上 wǎn/wǎnshang *106*
night time 夜間 yèjiān *90*

nine 九 jiǔ *18*
nine points 九分 jiǔfēn *18*
nine-hundred and ten 九百一十 jiǔbǎiyīshí *18*
nineteen 十九 shíjiǔ *18*
ninety-eight 九十八 jiǔshíbā *18*
ninth 第九 dìjiǔ *18*
ninth (of a month) 九號 jiǔhào *18*
no 不是 bùshì *35*; 不 bù *60*
no longer 不再 bùzài *53*
no matter 哪怕 nǎpà *109*
no matter how 多麼 duōme *31, 87*
no one knows 誰知道 shéi zhīdào *61*
no problem 沒問題/沒事 méi wèntí/méishì *81*
no question 沒問題 méi wèntí *81*
noon 午/中午 wǔ/zhōngwǔ *104*
not 不 bù *60*
not able to eat 吃不下 chībuxià *105*
not at all 不客氣 bùkèqi *60*
not full/not enough to eat 吃不飽 chībubǎo *105*
not in 不在 bùzài *72*
not necessarily 不見得 bùjiànde *54*
not to be 不是 bùshì *35*
not well 生病 shēngbìng *38*
not yet 還沒 háiméi *81*
November 十一月 shíyīyuè *19*
now 現在 xiànzài *72*; 今 jīn *91*
nowadays 如今 rújīn *91*
number 號碼 hàomǎ *94*
number nine 九號 jiǔhào *18*
number ten 十號 shíhào *94*

O
obviously 明明 míngmíng *95*
October 十月 shíyuè *19*
often 時時/不時 shíshí/bùshí *89*
OK! 好啊! hǎo a *22*
old 老 lǎo *43*
old friend 老朋友 lǎopéngyǒu *48*
old woman 老婆婆 lǎopópo *43*
older brother 哥/哥哥 gē/gēge *67*
older sister 姐/姐姐 jiě/jiějie *68*
older sister and younger brother 姐弟 jiědì *69*

List of Radicals

— 1 stroke —

1 一 one
2 丨 down
3 丶 dot
4 丿 left
5 乙 twist
6 亅 hook

— 2 strokes —

7 二 two
8 亠 lid
9 人 man
10 儿 legs
11 入 enter
12 八 eight
13 冂 borders
14 冖 crown
15 冫 ice
16 几 table
17 凵 bowl
18 刀 knife
19 力 strength
20 勹 wrap
21 匕 ladle
22 匚 basket
23 匸 box
24 十 ten
25 卜 divine
26 卩 seal
27 厂 slope
28 厶 cocoon
29 又 right hand

— 3 strokes —

30 口 mouth
31 囗 surround
32 土 earth
33 士 knight
34 夂 follow
35 夊 slow
36 夕 dusk
37 大 big
38 女 woman
39 子 child
40 宀 roof
41 寸 thumb
42 小 small
43 尢 lame
44 尸 corpse
45 屮 sprout
46 山 mountain
47 川 river
48 工 work
49 己 self
50 巾 cloth
51 干 shield
52 幺 coil
53 广 lean-to
54 廴 march
55 廾 clasp
56 弋 dart
57 弓 bow

58 彐 pig's head
59 彡 streaks
60 彳 step

— 4 strokes —

61 心 heart
62 戈 lance
63 戶 door
64 手 hand
65 支 branch
66 攴 knock
67 文 pattern
68 斗 peck
69 斤 axe
70 方 square
71 无 lack
72 日 sun
73 曰 say
74 月 moon
75 木 tree
76 欠 yawn
77 止 toe
78 歹 chip
79 殳 club
80 毋 don't
81 比 compare
82 毛 fur
83 氏 clan
84 气 breath
85 水 water
86 火 fire
87 爪 claws
88 父 father
89 爻 crisscross
90 爿 bed
91 片 slice
92 牙 tooth
93 牛 cow
94 犬 dog

— 5 strokes —

95 玄 dark
96 玉 jade
97 瓜 melon
98 瓦 tile
99 甘 sweet
100 生 birth
101 用 use
102 田 field
103 疋 bolt
104 疒 sick
105 癶 back
106 白 white
107 皮 skin
108 皿 dish
109 目 eye
110 矛 spear
111 矢 arrow
112 石 rock
113 示 sign
114 禸 track
115 禾 grain

116 穴 cave
117 立 stand

— 6 strokes —

118 竹 bamboo
119 米 rice
120 糸 silk
121 缶 crock
122 网 net
123 羊 sheep
124 羽 wings
125 老 old
126 而 beard
127 耒 plow
128 耳 ear
129 聿 brush
130 肉 meat
131 臣 bureaucrat
132 自 small nose
133 至 reach
134 臼 mortar
135 舌 tongue
136 舛 discord
137 舟 boat
138 艮 stubborn
139 色 color
140 艸 grass
141 虍 tiger
142 虫 bug
143 血 blood
144 行 go
145 衣 gown
146 襾 cover

— 7 strokes —

147 見 see
148 角 horn
149 言 words
150 谷 valley
151 豆 flask
152 豕 pig
153 豸 snake
154 貝 cowrie
155 赤 red
156 走 walk
157 足 foot
158 身 torso
159 車 car
160 辛 bitter
161 辰 early
162 辵 halt
163 邑 city
164 酉 wine
165 釆 sift
166 里 village

— 8 strokes —

167 金 gold
168 長 long
169 門 gate
170 阜 mound
171 隶 grab

172 隹 dove
173 雨 rain
174 青 green
175 非 wrong

— 9 strokes —

176 面 face
177 革 hide
178 韋 walk off
179 韭 leeks
180 音 tone
181 頁 head
182 風 wind
183 飛 fly
184 食 food
185 首 chief
186 香 scent

— 10 strokes —

187 馬 horse
188 骨 bone
189 高 tall
190 髟 hair
191 鬥 fight
192 鬯 mixed wine
193 鬲 cauldron
194 鬼 ghost

— 11 strokes —

195 魚 fish
196 鳥 bird
197 鹵 salt
198 鹿 deer
199 麥 wheat
200 麻 hemp

— 12 strokes —

201 黃 yellow
202 黍 millet
203 黑 black
204 黹 embroider

— 13 strokes —

205 黽 toad
206 鼎 tripod
207 鼓 drum
208 鼠 mouse

— 14 strokes —

209 鼻 big nose
210 齊 line-up

— 15 strokes —

211 齒 teeth

— 16 strokes —

212 龍 dragon
213 龜 tortoise

— 17 strokes —

214 龠 flute